The Funeral Game
NOEL MONAHAN

salmonpoetry

Other Books by Noel Monahan

Opposite Walls. Salmon Publishing, 1991.

Snowfire. Salmon Publishing, 1995.

Curse of the Birds. Salmon Publishing, 2000.

for Anne

Published in 2004 by
Salmon Publishing Ltd.,
Cliffs of Moher, County Clare, Ireland
Website: www.salmonpoetry.com
Email: info@salmonpoetry.com

ISBN 1 903392 12 8

Cover artwork: *A Cottage Garden* by Walter Osborne. Reproduced with the
permission of the National Gallery of Ireland.
Cover design & typesetting: Siobhán Hutson
Printed in Ireland by ColourBooks

il mezzo del cammin di nostra vita
midway along the journey of our life.

The Divine Comedy — Inferno
DANTE

Acknowledgements

Acknowledgement is due to the editors of the following in which a number of these poems first appeared:

Poetry Ireland Review, Poetry New Zealand, Poetry Scotland, Books Ireland, Cork Literary Review, The Spark, Artwords 2001, Cavan Anthology, Cathal Buí Anthology 2001, Clifden Anthology 2002, The Backyards Of Heaven (An Anthology Of Contemporary Poetry from Ireland, and Newfoundland & Labrador), The Anglo Celt, Bank of Ireland Out To Lunch, THE SHOp, An Guth, Flying Colours Poetry Festival Dublin, and *The Edgeworth Papers*, Vol. VII.

The poem, "The Funeral Game", won the inaugural SeaCat National Poetry Award, organised by Poetry Ireland.

Some of these poems have been broadcast on Rattlebag, RTE Radio1, Shannonside/Northern Sound and Dublin City Anna Livia FM.

Thanks to Tom MacIntyre, Heather Brett, Catriona O'Reilly and Cavan County Council for their encouragement.

Contents

3 — *The Funeral Game*

I Want To Invite You In

I want to invite you in.
The door has no house,
It stands in a field
With a mirror hanging
      From the sky.

Birds fly in from nowhere.
You can see a mirage of song dance,
You can hear their wings
Quench the seven stars
      As dawn begins.

1

Crane Dance

Crane Dance

She danced down the road,
Long red boots reaching
The feathers of her thighs,
Sprung a flight, a slow lift
Above the sycamore,
Croaking to the rain
In the drowsy clouds.

His screech was wild,
He cut across Dagger's Hill,
Stripping dust from the road,
Mapping the grey noise.

Falling towards one another,
Bowing and bobbing
They clung to the wind,
Looped their ice age tongues,
Gave voice, wild inflected shrieks,
Dancing all the way back
To a first scribble and screech.

And the lightning in the rain
Of their feathers blossomed into colour,
Quickening to the touch, legs trailing,
She bared her under feathers,
Lunging upwards he sealed
The first words in her pouch.

The Fields Are With Me

The fields are with me,
Filling every dream. Bushes
Grow inside, red berry winters,
Blossom white summers ...
Gates hang from ivy piers,
Half standing.

My limbs are branches holding
Snow in last year's nest,
Roads run in my veins
To roof, chimney and moon,
To every window, door and gable,
Once upon a time roads .....

With grass creeping through the walls,
An electric pole stands alone
Stripped of its light,
Faces talk from the fields,
Chant names of all who once lived here
And now lie dead.

The fields are with me.
Bushes burn inside,
Blazing memories, talking tongues .....

The Black Pig

She has spent her entire life out here,
Sun by day, moon by night
Shadows hovering everywhere.

Night fall.
Trees talk freely in their sleep,
Every leaf a tongue to dampen:
Her mossy ears, eyebrows of cut-hay,
Gaping fieldmouth of stones,
Pig's whiskers, tail in tatters.

Four legs astraddle,
Fed from clay, watered by river,
Rooted between places and time,
Alone dreamer and dreamed.

Morning leans over her shoulder.
Whins saddle her back, she has only
To open her eyes to see her own wreckage,
Scattered entrails of roads,
The rain eating her heart out.

Goat From Inchmore

I bring home the goat I met
On Inchmore. His cruel habits,
Nimble feet and horns are mine.

I follow him, slouching behind briars,
Getting nearer and nearer
That island inside me.

I climb the walls — old walls,
Brown and mossy...
Stare at the fields of Ballinroey.

I wrap his hide about me,
Rank smell — old reprobate,
Beard down to my toes.

Shadowman

The bush was in his head,
Thorns in his eyes, leaves,
Ears listening for the wind.

Rooted between two fields,
Summer sang white
On his shoulders,

Airiness of winter,
Feelings cold as clay,
Haws in his hands for the birds.

The Brown Hare

The brown hare sits in a chair,
Sharing her secrets with the fire.
Hare lip trembles,
Grey sods blaze away,
Blue smoke rises.

She stares at me,
Offers a paw,
Tells me to forage for the moonlight
In the field
Overlooking the fire.

The brown hare is homesick
For wind and heather,
She eyes the flames,
Tears up the chimney,
And vanishes into the cool of the moon.

Banished Faces

Faces of deities
      Out there in the clouds,
Old faces
      Long since banished:

     Mercury —
            Venus —
                    Mars —
                         Saturn —

Now that they've gone,
We hear them in our sleep,

     Chattering
        Like old streams
     Running back to childhood,

          Drifting

             With the wind

                To polish the snow.

Glangevlin Prayer

Send me back in time
To where the old woman
Lifts her face from the stones.

Let me scoop the bog-water,
Wash my face
In the froth of the fall.

Give me time to find the lost child
In these hard sliced rocks
Where wool is caught on stone.

Send me the dreams
From the lone bush in the hollymeadow,
Let the words rain down on the page.

The Nest

A woman at my pillow
Shakes me out of sleep
To look back
At a hovel of sticks and straw
Wedged in the top branches of a high tree.

Chicks bob their heads,
Make a meal of a mouse,
The mother owl folds her sleeves
Into the moon,
The dream is mirrored across the morning.

Rainbow Woman

I am a temple
Cast in the mould of rain.

My shoulder blades
Are stained glass.

When I stretch
I arc the covenant.

My feet are made
For walking on water.

I am the lady of the wilderness,
My words are tongues of fire.

My ears are full
Of listening.

Lady Of Drumlane

She hasn't quite gone
From the ivy window.
I find her alone, listening to the rain

Ghostly on churchyard slabs,
See her run through tangled reeds
Down to a neighbouring lake

Where grey clouds come in
And briars come home
Leafy with roses and thorns.

Night Frog

A frog fell
From the coal bucket,
Jumped about the floor,
Opened his pink mouth and said:
You're glad I came out of the dark.

The room shook with his croak,
Pots and jars talked,
Chairs and tables walked,
The central heating gurgled:
Hop hup my little frog
Hop hup again ....

And the bewildered little fellow
Sat in front of me,
Small hands, long feet,
His eyes were cold,
He couldn't stand the heat,

Frog peeled off a black vest,
Then a green one ... a yellow one.
Frog danced naked in the hallway,
Waited by the door,
Till I set him free
Into the moon and stars.

Our Dreams Are Asking Us to Re-Member

There's a crayfish in my sleep,
All legs, he wades along a riverbed,
Past gates on water hinges
To moonfields of stone and sand.

Blankets of starlings — curtain blue
Sing to Orpheus on my pillow,
Hold rock concerts in a field of stars:
We are the world — We are the people

The wolf at my bedroom window
Is howling to the moon,
His piercing eyes
Reaching for Apollo.

Waking up,
I try to re-member my name.
Good Morning Mr. Crayfish,
Good Morning Mr. Starling,
Good Morning Mr. Wolf.

The Snow Ghost

The snow ghost
Is predictably white
And hardly recognisable.

She's an aristocrat,
Enthroned in drifts
With the moon under her feet
And the stars in her hair.

She speaks well,
Asterisks of words
Melt on her lips in the night.

Sometimes she's old,
A shawl of bones
Racing past the window.
But always white,
Long before colour crossed our minds.

You might say
The snow ghost
Is predictably part of me,
Dreaming alongside me
In the anonymous snow.

2

The Colosseum

Threnody For Rosie

Up the Plastic Mountains,
Down the Beercan Hills,
Finance Minister in the parlour
Counting raisins in his scones,
Civil Servants all gone blind
With Euro on their mind.
Farewell my lovely Rosie
A hundred thousand times farewell.

Some work, more mouse about
The Internet through fields of files,
Will anyone ring a TD for a favour?
Hall of mirrors, hall of horrors,
Tribunal blues, tribunal greens and yellows.
Off to jail - Back out again- Nothing done, less to do.
Farewell my lovely Rosie
A hundred thousand times farewell.

Satellite dishes on the gables,
Women wanting to be priests
Priests want to marry,
Does anyone ever mention God?
O little town of Bethlehem
Do your best for the local football team.
Farewell my lovely Rosie
A hundred thousand times farewell.

The fields are falling from the hills,
Farmers out of pocket, Celtic Tiger
Burning bright — gave no light,
Darkness falling — who's to care?
Pope screaming in the electric chair,
Paparazzi everywhere.
Farewell my lovely Rosie
A hundred thousand times farewell.

The Bacchae

They cross the street like outlaws,
Cauls on their heads, blood aprons,
Mobile phones in their pockets.
Saunter into a pub, call for soup and sandwiches —
Bark at one another to pass the salt...sauce...

Morphia Murphy blows smoke through her ears,
Sunday Sally farts, the cheeks of her arse
Laugh on the chair.
Pool-balls break, all smiles in the mirror
Across at the men on the other side,
Drop their heads into the soup,
Drum on the side of the counter with their feet.

We are the Bo-Peeps ready to knife the sheep.
We watch them inching towards the blade,
Hear the thumping of their hearts,
Slit them open, hose them down,
Shroud them in frost in the deep freeze,
Shout to outnoise the meat-saw,
Wheel the ice, push the hooks forward,
Waltz the meat-crane ... walkman blaring.

We're the mad *hoores* of this town,
Wild drunk at weekends,
Dancing on tables, hunting in packs
At discos and in bars.
We are sisters of the kill
Studded noses, ears and lips.
We know the inside of blood
Bulky heifers bleeding in a line,
Bulls stripped to the bone.

All that blood makes us horny...
Sunday Sally shags the boner in the loo,
Jacinta ates raw flesh when she's on the kill,
Praise the Lord and pass the salt,
The forecast isn't good: There's blood in the rain
Coming down from the hills.

The Colosseum

We are one with Caesar in the Hogan Stand,
Waiting for the sun to bounce,
Screaming at Jesus with the county jersey on,
Shouting for his blood, his living flesh:
Play the game ... pass the bloody ball.
And in the communion of Chablis or flasks of tea
We send up our sighs at half-time:
God help us should the wind change.

Second half, eyes back and forth,
Forwards down on all fours, someone is carted off,
Someone is taken off, Jesus grabs the moon
Stops — looks — kicks it over the wood,
We rise to our feet ... roars ... cheers ... blood red faces,
At one with the tribe and Caesar on our side.

Bank Holiday Weekend

It is night
Dark awakens the headlights
On The Mad Cow Roundabout,
I see Isaac Newton driving furiously
A Ford Mondeo
Hurry! Hurry! Hurry! .....

p u n o
r
a b o u t s   o
h
s   t
e
r o   r o
u   u
n   n
d   d

a   n   d

U
P   THE   M   50
D
O
W
N   THE   N   4

Away! Away! Away! .....
Heading for Slieve Cuilcagh
To see the trees walk, hear the birds talk ...

Cars overheat — engines go on fire,
Cars fall apart — falling through broken wire,
Weeds laughing in the side mirror,
Sheep grinning from the hills,
The drive shaft drops ...
Tyres — wheels — and axles ...
Quickstep down the slopes .....

Water gushes up,
River spews and spits.
Car sinks.

It is night,
The Eye of the moon half shut,
Isaac Newton's face looks up from the river
All the colours of the spectrum ....
Took a wrong turn at The Glan Gap
Hurry! Hurry! Hurry! .....
The rest is fluxions.

Mirror At Dawn

Sheep falling asleep
In the twilight of blue grass
Above the woollen sky.

Windmills On Slieve Rushen

From the roadside,
They look like a pair of swimmers,
Hands slicing the blue
Between heaven and mountain heather.

As I near the summit
They transform:
Two Idols — Giant Beetles,
Mounted on pillars, sunk in shadow,
Harvesting the wind
With nose propellers,
Playing airport music to a pylon altar,
Spiked candles ... steel flowers ...

Morning Observations

I'm looking out a window
At the backs of houses,
Fenestration of indifference, double-glaze, old teak ...
Chimney pots, red, yellow ..... more
Green with grass and weed,
Grey smiles from the slates above.

A few towels hang from a string in the garden
Waiting for a breath of wind. New clouds fall
Into action. A seagull flies past -
Ivy is climbing over oil tanks, garden sheds ...
The garden gate is beginning to rust.
The garden path gets lost in the grass.

Some child kicks a ball against a wall,
A hiker, complete with rucksack
Stops to fix his earphones,
Another seagull flies past -
The geraniums in the window-box
Are scarcely standing on last year's stilts,
A woman walks home from Mass.
The hiker retraces his tracks,
He must have forgotten something.

Accordion Player

for Martin Donohoe

He sways from side to side,
Feet of a dancer under the table,
Loving every button, every press
And draw of the bellows,
Laughs to himself
In hayfields of jigs and reels,
Free-reeding with the Kinnegad Slasher,
Past drinking men on the edge
Of their stools,
To cliffs and gulls
In mist and fog and smoke,
Folding and unfolding the grief of the sea.

Meadow Of Storm

It was the last rattle of the bucket,
You could tell
By the look on the red hen,
The cry of the curlew.

It was a storm in the wilderness.
If you listen long enough
To the wind in the sycamores,
You'll see it swipe at the hay
And the hay-cocks shake with laughter.

First the sunhats rise,
Then the hay-cocks, like bald monks and nuns,
Step wildly through the fields
For the last hay-dance.
Lazarus late out of bed
Saw a camera flash, or was it lightning?

The winds of change rip at the butts,
Hay-cocks turn to comets,
Ghosts'beards, longtails, fossil grass
Are swept over the trees, across the hills,
Dipping and rising,
An Empire of hay on the move,
Heading out to the aftergrass of heaven.

Interim

(after Bede)

This is where we are –
Waiting for a new song,
Ever since the statues toppled
From their pedestals
And ghosts walk about the aisle
At Christ The King.

At Christ The King
You get far more graces
Waiting for a hand-tap on the shoulder
Or for another single sparrow
To fly in one door — out another.

Visiting Relations

The house is one great grandmother
Holding us together when we arrive,
Shaking hands with our shadows,
Settling us down on chairs.

Aunt Bella holds her breath pouring tea,
A spoon makes china music
In the sugar bowl, the milk jug swallows.
Aunt Agnes twitches her elephant ears
Patiently listening to my father going on
About The Irish Soldiers:
Eaten alive in the Congo.

A lull in conversation,
Our eyes travel the blue of the carpet,
Past forest green curtains to the snow
Of the tablecloth. The cathedral clock
Strikes every half hour.

Our great grandmother falls asleep
In the foliage of her armchair.
And I'm forever watching the girl from next door,
Long red hair thrown back on the sofa,
Her warm legs beside me.

The Tent Makers

for Thomas Pettit

It was our tepee, a makeshift tent,
Cartwheel and axle lodged in the ground,
Covered in old sheets, raincoat and blanket,
With a ring of straw to lie on.

From here we sailed to Colchis
Past gooseberry bushes
Where Harpies gobbled fruit,
Saw Talos in an old plough rising out of a ditch.

Summers were sunny long,
In the halcyon days of the haggart.
Time let us dream.
We counted dust specks in a shaft of light,
Made promises on wishbones,
Held seashells to our ears,
Listening to the shape of the wind.

The farm gathered round us.
Green calves, blue lambs,
All sang to the tune
Of a milkbottle rattling morning.
Bob the horse galloped past on stilts.

We waited in ambush for buffalo
Words tumbled, we spoke Apache
Roared like lions, howled like wolves,
Climbed over winter logs,
Speared crocodiles in a lake of weeds,
Shouting and shooting at everything and anything.

The wheel turned,
We lost sight of the Golden Fleece.
Trees leafed, flowered, berried .....
Holly boys and ivy girls went sliding in the snow
To kill the wren.

We're Getting There

for Kevin Lavelle

Our shoulders rise and fall
In the trench below the bungalow
And you repeat for the umpteenth time
We're getting there.
I crawl out of the clay for a break,
Go traipsing up and down,
Catching the snow in my coat.
You hack away at your Golgotha of stones.

It's Spring but Winter hasn't left us yet.
We pause to take our breath,
Look to Sliabh Glah constantly changing,
Talk of climbing her sometime soon.
A robin looks with disappointment,
Not a single worm in sight.
The dog barks at a passing crow.

You are all shoulders
And determined to keep the line straight,
Lay the black water- pipes.
I talk of some football match,
Anything to distract. The snow starts
To fill the trench, shroud the water- pipes
And you repeat for the umpteenth time
We're getting there.

Flashback

Sometimes I see primroses
In green moss along a ditch,
Bees still drowsy after winter,
A farmer spreading fodder,
The East wind at his back.

And Our Lady glares at me
From the landing window,
Primroses in a jampot at her feet,
Two candles flickering.

On The Scullery Rail

A line of rejection from the past.
Sandals spattered in tar,
Black boots deadly pale at the toe
After the winter snow,
White high heels separated,
Resigned to live apart.

The idle line occupies me.
I am drawn to their little height
On the wooden rail,
Clay crumbs at their heels,
Mildew on their soles.

Corpus Christi Procession

Down the hill they come. Forever
In sunlight, past Flaherty's and Clyne's
With altars out to the Sacred Heart,
Big peony roses, candles flickering on brass.

Christ's representatives are here:
Children of Mary throb with pagan blood,
The Legion of Mary is on the march,
Men, bald heads, Sunday suits,
Await the kiss of holy water,
First Communion Girls carry roses,
A world where angels pass

The Market House draped in bunting.
The choir deep in the throes of hymns,
O touch our hearts, so cold and so ungrateful,
    An altar-boy walks backwards,
Swinging a thurible before a priest
In a canopy of linen and lace.

Back to the hill for Benediction.
The monstrance of the sun rises above the town,
All heads bow to
The phantasmagoria of *Kyria, Gloria, Sanctus* ...
The whole place is silent
You can almost hear the men in the next parish
Talk football in their sleep.

The School Piano

When the tuner stripped down
The piano frame,
Before the school reopened,
He found a ball of hay and leaves
Hanging
    Between E flat and G.

No blind mice within
To face the music in September.
Only the silent song
Of a lived-in nest
The mice gone ... other things to do.

All Day Long

At school we see
Ink spilt on the floor.
Children get bored
Counting, conjugating verbs ....
All day long.

You never know
When some disappear
You never know
Where to find them.

Teachers are patient,
See with their eyes.
Children, not easily tamed,
See with their hearts,
And are made to sit in rows,
In blue and navy uniforms.

How can you know
When some disappear?
How can you know
Where to find them?

Principals, Deputy Principals,
Constantly counting the children,
Mornings and afternoons
Names and numbers put on files.

One never knows
When they go missing
One never knows
Where to find them.

3

The Funeral Game

The Funeral Game

That winter we came to terms with death.
Every shoe-box was a coffin
For anything small and dead
And we wrapped them in calicoes, velvets ...

We grabbed hats, coats, umbrellas,
From the hallway to dress as mourners,
Someone struck an iron girder in the hay-shed
To sound the funeral bell,
John Joe beat the dead march on a saucepan.

We held wakes, issued death certificates
To old crows, kittens, chickens ...
Lined the graves with stones,
Erected crosses with ash sticks.

We pretended to cry, struggled with Latin prayers,
Filled the wet graves in the clover field,
Genuflected in the direction of a whin bush,
The rain pelting down,
We left by a side-gap,
Back to the hay-shed for tea, bread, butter ...
For all who travelled long journeys.

An File Ar Leaba A Bháis

Táim ag fáil bháis go deo na ndeor
Le fada is ceithre chéad bliain anuas,
Im luí idir na bráillíní,
Balcaisí ar an gcathaoir, bróga ar an urlár
Na bastúnaí taobh amuigh ag ithe na liopaí
Ag fanacht le m'anáil dheireanach.

Táim chomh hainbhiosach le sicín
Gan ceann ag rith tríd an chlós.
Ní imeoidh an fheannóg ó phost na leapan,
Tá mo theach ina chónra,
Is bíonn le rá agam an méid atá ráite
Ón uair gur imigh an bhó bhuí as bainne
Is an óinseach ag aoir ar an amadán.

Valsálann na spéirmná tharam,
Cainteach, caointeach igcónaí i bpunc,
Cheistigh siad díom cá raibheas,
Is d'fhreagair mé go raibh mo bheanchéile
Amuigh san ollmhargadh ag síor díol mo dhánta,
Iad á gcaitheamh ar chúl na mbus
Iad á gcur i gcló ar chartáin bainne,
Is go bhfilleann sí igcónaí leis an gceist úd,
Cé a cheannódh dán?

Tá an doctúir ag síorsciolladh m'ae,
Tógfaidh mé aon leigheas
Seachas Dr. James's Powders, adeirim.
Tá mo mháilín domlais chomh mór le balún,
Táim chomh torrach le torathar an bháis
Mar a ghabhadh ón Spiorad Naomh.
Cuir duine éigin e-mail go Dia,
atharmacspioradnaomh @ neamh.com

Go dtaga ríocht na mbalún,
Tabhair dúinn inniu iomas gréine,
Umhlóimid ós comhair na haltóra
Agus bás in Éirinn do chách … Alleluia … Alleluia …

Cleachtaím mo shochraid ó thús go deireadh,
Crónán na gcléir ag fógairt an tSaltair,
Na síciatraí, corrmhúinteoir, screach ó na maighdeana
Is cruacheist an adhlacóra — an iomad daoine ionam
Á gcur san uaigh, ach is iomaí duine ag Dia
Agus is mó mé i mise ag triall go mall go reilig Ghleann
na bPúcaí.

Is olc an chríoch a chuir mé orm féin
Ag fáil bháis le ceithre chéad bliain anuas,
Nocht an taibhse dom ar maidin,
Nach raibheas ach ag fáil bháis im chodhladh,
Aisling bhréige ag ionsaí, stair litríochta
Ina luí go trom orm.
Chnámhaigh mé an dán seo den uaigh atá ionam
Agus beidh mé ag éisteacht go deo leis an gcré nua.

The Poet On His Death Bed

I'm forever dying in bed
For the last four hundred years,
Bundled between the sheets
Frippery on the chair, boots on the floor
And all them vulgarians out there
Waiting for the words to die on my lips.

I'm as unconscious as a headless chicken
Running round the yard.
The hooded crow won't leave the bedpost,
My house is my coffin
And I've been saying what's been said to death,
Since the yellow cow went dry,
And the pots and pans collided in the wind.

A bevy of skywomen waltz past me on the wall,
All whingers from God's old time,
Intent on having me remember the future.
I tell them I sent my wife out
To sell my poems in the supermarket,
Fling them on the backs of buses,
Have them printed on milk cartons
But she returns with the age old question,
Who would buy a poem now?

The doctor is forever scolding my liver,
I will take any medication but *Dr. James's Powders*,
My gallbladder has ballooned,
I'm as pregnant as the monster of death
Like I've conceived a god or two.
Someone called a Carmelite, had him e-mail God:
fathersonandholyghost @ heaven. com
Thy kingdom of balloons will come,

Thy will be done with searching
The potato stalks for sun bubbles,
Wrap thy belly in red flannel
And wait for the dead-by-date
From the doctor.....Alleluia.....Alleluia.

I'm hell bent on rehearsing my funeral,
The lugubrious clerics maundering the Psalter,
Sophisters, the odd teacher, shrieks from
The young girls and the undertaker
Puzzled by the thought of having
To bury my multiple self....
Ego..... I and Me
They'll never hold us in Glenafooka graveyard.

But the end as expected never comes,
All the dying and I'm still not dead,
Of late I discovered I was only half asleep,
Chasing the wrong ghost round the haggart,
Too much of the anorexic poems,
The bare bones pared down to molecules,
The diet of words that left me wasting,
Naked in the bed all these years.
Till at last I found the grave in myself
And now I must listen to the clay.

The Blessing Of The Graves

Some walked — cars purred
Down the Granardkille road
To the graveyard,
Labyrinth of crosses,
Chiselled names, dates, phrases from scripture:
O death, where is thy sting?
R.I.P.s everywhere.

We stood between two worlds,
The living looking in on the dead.
Rain pored down, umbrellas coloured the evening,
The priest walked to the brow of the hill,
Read prayers into a hand-mike,
Swallows criss-crossed,
A child took white stones from one grave
To place on another, his mother cautioned him
And he sulked.
Someone tripped over a clump of grass.

Rain continued,
You could hear families breathe,
Huddled about their graves,
Hoping to see through clay and stone,
Touch cheeks, hold hands once more,
Talk .....
But no one spoke.
Only the priest raised his voice
And we befriended vague shadows - memories.

Limbo

Once my father said
He planted the unborn bones
Of a child that wasn't to be,
Released them
Into an unmade grave,
Marked the spot with an undressed stone
Above the wild raspberry canes
In the clover field.

And every time he passed,
He looked to see
If the feet had taken root,
If the fingers had grown
And pushed away the stone.

Between Two Worlds

That morning we heard
The usual door squeaks,
Tap water running, kettle on the boil,
Rain beating against the window, lambs bleating.

But you were listening elsewhere,
Out of tune with love,
Caught between two worlds
Your hands still warm from pulling a calf
That refused to leave the womb,
Triggered something cold and dark inside
And drove you to the shadow lands
Of your own back garden
To war against yourself.

Was there no song or prayer
To raise your heart?
No dream or poem or child's hosanna
To lift you up to a saving grace.
Were the fields your hell?
That you should turn your back
On the surprise of April
Primroses on the ditch, cowslips, buttercups
In the meadow, birds building their nests.

We sat dumbfounded.
Cows not milked, calves not fed,
The dog at the door, the cat by the fire.
Buckets rattled,
Spade, shovel, grape ...
Walked about the yard
Ghosts came from nowhere
Barefooted, hooded in hoarfrost,
Older than the fields
To walk behind your coffin.

The Snow Has Something To Say

Once upon a time
There was a song in the snow
And the song sang itself to sleep.

When the bee heard the snow sing
He dared to leave the hive,
Flying, falling through frozen petals,
Climbing snowmountains far and near,
Over the hillsnow blazing white,
Far white, far away .....

And there were blackbirds in another world
Scraping up dead leaves,
With beaks sharp enough to bleed the wind.
And when they heard the snowmusic buzzing,
They came from under the trees,
Flying low — a black river meandering
Across linenfields ... wheatfields... moonfields ...
And the blackbirds grew mad and madder
With the snowsong and all the while the white
Till at last they found the bee
In the long butter of the hedge
Soaking up the honey.

The blackbirds, old masters of the hedge-school,
Sat around, instructing him on his erring ways,
How foolish he was to leave the hive
For out-of-season flowers :
Heaven knows what you and I believe
You can't be listening to the snow,
It has nothing to say.
But the bee was exuberantly happy
In the trancewhite... sleepwhite... silent white ...
Pure cold light of the moon.

There was a silence before somebody
Said something or nothing at all.
And in the white of a snowflake
The bee turned into a fish, his wings, fins,
Each liquid breath, a word melting on his lips.
Swimming beyond oceans of snowflake,
Twisting and turning in the new excitement.
And the blackbirds, now hardly black at all
Scuttled across the snow
Back to the scrawny leaves under the trees.

The snows of yesterday have something to say:
They remember the secrets of water.
The sorrow of a snow song ever calling:
Out of the drifts I cry unto you,
All the while I whiten
I know my own melting power.

Once upon a time
There was a song in the snow
And the song sang itself to sleep.

Abraham And Isaac

When Abraham saw the lightning
He didn't wait for the thunder,
Yoked his mule, grabbed Isaac
His much loved son
And headed for the mountain of Moriah.

It was a hard climb,
Abraham's soul in disarray:
Flash-backs ... noises ... strange colours .....
Remote from his feelings,
Soul-searching beyond the reach of reason.

Father and son sitting quietly
Face to face in the half-shut eye of the moon.
Flies swarm above Abraham's sweaty shirt,
His shoulder stiff as a stone,
The knife drawn –

What if the angel arrived late
And Abraham knifed his son?
Would he be tried for filicide?
HEADLINES ON EVERY NEWSPAPER
Much talk in the small towns.

And what did young Isaac make of all this?
At first I was unaware of the funeral game,
Much relieved to see the angel arrive on time,
Dad settled for a ram instead,
Everyone was happy, especially Mum.

Agamemnon And Iphigenia

It can happen again.
Foggy days and nights at Aulis,
Not a breath of wind
And the horse trading begins...

Much talk of sacrifice, the gods demanding
Iphigenia, the child,
Her father Agamemnon with his eyes
Fixed on Troy.

Agamemnon, thinking himself nearly a god,
Prays: *Blessed be the blood*,
The crowd stands round,
Long faces, sealed lips, pale silence.

Blade flicker ——— splatter of blood,
Daughter lies open on the altar,
Her cry echoes:
     In the black of nowhere,

Her blood rushing in all their veins.
The wind rises, men sail to war,
     It happened a long time ago.
It happens again and again.

Shantemon

Nine times I walked
Round your fingers in the snow.
Black bushes stooped with winter beards,
Skeletal pines creaked out of the blue.

Your fingers beckoned, I leaned
Against the shoulder of your thumb,
Staring at your long life lines, the blotchy roses,
Marks of woe, beneath a glove of snow.

Your stone-age hand took hold of me,
Your frozen fingers played on the wind
A winter tune that opened the mouths
Of every stone in every field in Shantemon.

Christmas Yawned In Waterlane

Christmas yawned in Waterlane
Icicles hung from a lamp-post,
Holly grief and holy leaf
Goose and turkey
        donkeycarted into town.

Carol morning, ghostly night
Men and women, scarves and caps
Went sleepy by to Mass,
Children's noses flat against the glass
Of Larry's toyshop window.

Train-set in the long ago
        Went blue
                and red
and yellow,
A monkey danced inside a cage
Mrs.Reilly vacuum-cleaned the snow
Outside her moonly half-lit door.

Christmas yawned in Waterlane
Cruets rattled on a tray,
Carol morning, ghostly night
Goose and turkey
        donkeycarted into town.

Three Wild Women

Three wild women:
Jane, Molly and Winnie came to town,
Good looking — in flowery robes,
One with fire and two with ice.

They ran the wise men home,
Got Mary up off her knees,
Rearranged the sacred furniture,
Uncaged the wren and robin,
Broke the cradle, burnt the boards,
One took the ass for a ride,
The other two milked the cow
And fed the child.

Three wild women:
Jane, Molly and Winnie came to town,
Good looking — in flowery robes,
One with fire and two with ice.

Ghost In The Crib

There was a ghost in the crib last Christmas,
Dressed as Santa, he stripped off his reds,
Danced in the pelt about the stable floor.

The child, being a wonder child,
Was polishing off a plate of robin and turnip,
When he shouted to his father:
Joseph! Joseph! Rumour has it:
Adam never bit the apple, only licked it.

That being said,
Everything had to come to a halt,
The star over the stable,
Alleluias, Glorias, Hosannas ..... all silent.

The ghost slipped back into his reds,
Grabbed a whip from the rafters,
Drove everyone out, sheep and shepherds
Back to the hills, the Holy Family went missing,
The donkey ran down the road, wise men after him.

Slamming the stable door,
Santa waved goodbye with a handkerchief,
Leaving the place eerie and deserted.

Mourners

They throng together,
Jostle for a place around the grave.
Their eyes fight wars,
Mouths speak with silence,
For this is the taming of the terrible
When the circle revels
In new dancing-places
And the dead one steps
Out of the ring
To walk in the tree tops
With the wind.

Post Card From Hades

You can tire of this place. Febrile rivers : Styx, Acheron, Lethe .....
And Charon the ferryman, always with his hand out for an obol.
Cerberus drooling at the mouth, continues to wag his tail
At new arrivals. Elysium, the only 5 Star Hotel and I can't
Afford it, have to settle for the dark and gloomy Tartarus with its
Big bronze gates. — no shower — no air conditioning,
    food terrible.
Truly hell if it weren't for the fields and fields of asphodel
Visible from my bedroom window. Tourist attractions are limited.
Daily tours to see Danaus' many daughters drawing water with
Leaking buckets and you can cable-car to the top of the hill
To view Sisyphus rolling his stone up
                only to have it roll down again.
It never rains — temperatures always roasting.
Hope to see you if I ever get back from here.

                                   Noel.